To Bowe,

my love – and hurry back soon for a real visit –

Mary Lou Lacy

a Woman wants God

by Mary Lou Lacy

a Woman wants God

JOHN KNOX PRESS
RICHMOND, VIRGINIA

The Library of Congress has catalogued this book as follows:

Lacy, Mary Lou.
A woman wants God. Richmond, John Knox Press [1959]
80 p. 22 cm.

1. Woman—Religious life. I. Title.

BV4527.L25 248 59–5120 ‡

Library of Congress

5947

To my mother
with thankfulness and love

Contents

A Woman wants God—but

Why is it, Lord, my soul does seek
  Companionship with Thee,
And yet my mind builds up a wall
  To block Thy Mind from me?

Why does my heart yearn desperately
  For closeness with Thy Heart,
And yet my will does not allow
  A yielding on my part?

Lord, I want Thee, truly want Thee,
  And know Thou wantest me.
Lord, help me, help me find the way
  To bind myself to Thee.

A WOMAN WANTS GOD. She wants Him because she knows deep within herself that she cannot live alone.

Enjoying the perfection of the Garden, Eve knew no loneliness. It was not only because Adam was there; it was because God walked there too. She knew His Presence in the darkness of the night when the presence of Adam, deep in sleep, seemed lost as a companion spirit. She experienced the power of His love when, in the brightness of the day, she marveled at the beauties of creation, the perfection of its plan, the vastness of its concept. She felt no insignificance as being a part of such a universe, for God had ordained her necessary to the completeness of His work. He had made her for a purpose, a purpose dear to Him, and He was with her in that relationship. She knew it; so Eve was never alone until—.

And ever since then woman has wanted God, has needed Him beyond expression because she cannot live alone. Entangled with the impediments of material possessions, cluttered with the complexities of a much involved culture, and endowed with the same qualities that caused Eve to hesitate and then choose evil instead of good, woman today still wants to have God, still cannot live alone.

Hard for her to understand is the fact that God is always wanting her, He is always more than seeking her, He is never beyond her ability to find Him if she will search. And she must search, not pretending to be different from what she really is, not shutting her eyes to her impatience, her pride, her desire to be like everyone else and yet a little exalted over her fellow men, but aware of all the imperfections that shut her off from God.

Yes, a woman wants God—but:

A woman is a busy, busy creature. She would like to have God in her life, if she could just accept Him and let that be the end of it until she desperately needs Him again.

A woman is a vain and prideful creature. How important it is to her to feel accepted by a special group, to *belong* socially! She cannot afford to maintain ideals for herself that might make her different. And always, where her children are concerned, she must give them every chance at happiness—

happiness dependent upon their having and doing and being just like the others in their all-important group.

A woman is a creature not completely free. She is not truly emancipated to the extent that she is independent of her husband. Financially and otherwise, he must be her master to some extent, and if God's presence in a woman's life causes a conflict of loyalties to occur, then surely these loyalties produce a stumbling block to true fellowship with God.

Yet, in spite of these obstacles and scores of others, a woman still must search for God until she finds Him, knows Him, uses Him completely in her life if she is never to be alone.

Together let us think, and seek, and ask. We will surely find Him if we try.

CHAPTER I

A Calendar, a Stocking, and an Armful of Flowers

LOOK AROUND YOU, woman, and you cannot but see three very ordinary things. At least they are ordinary in a woman's world, for where she dwells, one can almost always find a calendar, a pair of nylon stockings, and flowers.

The calendar marks the day's activities, decides the dates of checks, and serves as a counting guide for some important time to come. However else would a woman know whether it is the first or second Monday that she faces; how could she possibly tell how many more days the rapidly disappearing grocery money must be stretched; and how else could she keep straight the order of her varied interests? Oh, yes, you have a calendar close at hand, so look at it, woman; look at it and the days you've already checked off this week, this month, this year. Look at those days of your life and know that they'll never be yours again.

Not very long ago, a friend and I discovered similar physical troubles. Both of us found sudden peculiar growths in our bodies. We consulted the same physician, who prepared us for the same operation. As I fought my way back to consciousness, I could rejoice that only minor surgery had been necessary in my case. When my friend awoke she found that a great part of her body had been cut away. Just recently God put an end to her sufferings and took her to be forever with Himself.

But what about me? Now, each time I pass her house I find myself thinking, "What would she have done with today if it still belonged to her as it does to me?" Each time I see the bright, blonde pony-tail of her teen-age daughter bobbing in a crowd of high school heads I cannot but wonder, "What would she have talked about to Sally if she could speak today as I can?" Each time my heart goes out in sympathy to her husband in his loneliness, I say to myself, "What would today have meant if they could be together again?"

Now, look once more at your calendar, and consider the days of your lifetime that are gone; so many days when you and I were happy in the completeness of God's love, or so many days when we were miserable without Him; so many days when we pulled others down, or lifted them up—so many days—*gone*. Do you see what I'm trying to say? It is not "Be fearful, woman, it's later than you think," but "Wake up, you! Wake up, me! God has given us today. Let us make it really count, count for something lasting and real!"

Search, woman, search, and you'll eventually come up with this unchanging answer—the only thing in life that is lasting and real is God and His boundless love for those who want it. Everything else changes, everything else ends. Everything else will leave you alone.

And there is an urgency about our finding Him. Time does not wait for us to discover the Priceless Pearl; life does not stand still until we decide that what we are living for is not worth dying for. Think, woman, think each time you see a calendar; and say within your mind and heart, "I must be seeking God now."

A nylon stocking that a woman wears is never far from sight. You and I have accepted the miracle of this marvelous substance, rejoicing in its strength, taking its accessibility much for granted, and yet not really knowing very much about the processes that make it so desired.

"Will you stay here for Christmas?" I asked a new next-door neighbor. "Or will you go to your mother's home for the holidays?"

"Oh, no," the neighbor answered; "my husband has to work on Christmas Day, so we will stay right here."

"Work on Christmas? Doesn't the nylon plant shut down even for Christmas?" I couldn't believe it!

"They can't shut down," she patiently explained to me. "Once the flow of liquid nylon begins to move through the large pipes it would be disaster to stop it. It would cool and harden, clogging and ruining the machinery. They must keep the cables open, the nylon flowing, even on Christmas Day, for this is a continuous process."

How like a woman and her search for God! Once the channel between them is established, once she opens her heart and soul and life to His inpouring Spirit, then the connection must be continuous, the way open at all times. Woman cannot merely reach up whenever she feels the need and expect the channel to be clear and ready to bring God close to her. She will find it clogged with useless repetitions of meaningless words that seem to solidify and block her off. No, the channel must be always open, once woman becomes aware. It must be in full-time use as she gradually learns to take advantage of God's unending search for her by meeting Him along the way. Indeed this is a continuous process!

When sorrow came and dwelt with me,
 The bleakness of my heart
Cried out to God, and begged that He
 Would help me bear my part.

But later on, when joy was mine
 And life was sweet and gay,
I had no thought for Him Divine;
 I pushed Him far away.

Is God a service I can use
 When need of Him I see?
Or always mine because I choose
 To seek Him seeking me?

One day, as I passed the city hospital, I saw a woman walking rapidly toward the entrance. In her arm she held a bunch of long-stemmed gladioli which she was obviously taking to a sick friend.

"That's quite a common thing to see outside a hospital," you are no doubt thinking. Yes, it is, but this sight was not so usual. You see, in one arm the woman held the flowers—

but she had only one arm. The other arm was missing. Even in her imperfection and inadequacy she was being used as an instrument of beauty and joy—used as a blessing to someone else! That's just what happens to you and me when we finally become successful in our search for God. We don't become perfect—no, far from it. We offer our twisted, one-sided, pitifully distorted lives up to God and He loves us in spite of our unworthiness. He accepts us and then is able to use the weak instruments that we are for some real good to His other children; is able to take our ugliness and turn it into beauty for His own glory.

An urgency to find Him? Yes. A constancy in seeking Him? Yes. A joy in being wanted and used by Him once we give Him the chance? Oh, yes, yes, yes! A calendar, a stocking, and an armful of flowers.

CHAPTER II

To seek Him seeking Me

"And I tell you, Ask, and it will be given you; seek, and you will find; knock, and it will be opened to you. For every one who asks receives, and he who seeks finds, and to him who knocks it will be opened."

—LUKE 11:9-10 (R.S.V.)

IN WANTING GOD ENOUGH TO FIND HIM, to know Him, to receive His blessings, woman must learn to keep the channel open, to be in constant contact with God. So as she seeks, she strives to understand the meaning of prayer.

"Prayer," says the little child, "is asking God for things we need."

"No," says the father, worried, tired; "prayer is putting our responsibilities on God."

"I disagree," the young person says. "Prayer is becoming friends with Jesus, talking to Him, telling Him what we plan to do each day."

"Wait," warns the priest. "You are forgetting that prayer is confession of sin which no man can bear without God's forgiveness."

"You are wrong," says the musician. "True prayer is adoration, worship in its loftiest form."

But woman, once she really understands, is content to say, "Prayer is simply being with God and knowing it."

What breathing is to the body, praying is to the Christian life. Take away breath and the body is dead; take away prayer and the life is no longer Christian. For a woman to have God, prayer is essential. It is a relationship that must result from an eager expectancy, combined with definite honest effort on the part of anyone who wants to experience *togetherness* with God. Prayer must be practiced not so much with the discipline of perfection as with the discipline of love.

It is entirely true that at times we happen upon companionship with God through no premeditated desire on our part. The first crocus suddenly discovered can bring forth an, "Oh, God, thank You for this beautiful flower to make me know that spring will surely come!" The way you feel when you hold your soft precious baby for the first time, can cause you secretly to murmur, "God, You and I are truly in this thing together." And "One more chance is all I ask, God, and I promise things will be different," is our attitude as we try to bargain with God in a crucial time. One cannot possibly say that these sudden feelings for God are not prayers. But they most certainly are not enough for a woman who wants to learn to be with God in a completeness that assures her she will never be alone!

Have you ever ridden for several hours on a bus, train, or plane with a stranger sitting in the seat beside you? Sometimes you start a conversation and become friends. Sometimes you don't. You ride, side by side, for hours but there is no recognition between the two of you. Sitting in adjoining seats, you are worlds apart, even oblivious of the other's existence.

Now—have you ever traveled side by side with someone you love deeply, and gone for fifteen, twenty, or thirty minutes without saying a word? And yet because you are there together, nothing need be said. You don't get lonely, you don't get frightened, you don't even get bored. You are together and just being together is enough.

What would it be like if our seeking God were sincere enough to have Him with us constantly, every minute of every day, every night? What would it be like? It would be like prayer—seeking Him seeking us.

But prayer is something else too. In spite of the fact that sometimes just being with God is enough, other times we must go a little farther. We want to talk to Him and we have to know how.

Many people have described the several different elements that should go into a perfect prayer, but for you and me in our personal, single relationship to God they don't necessarily have to be included. If a prayer is sincere, it is human; and if it is human, it is not perfect. Jesus taught us to think of God as our Father. It is only natural that a child talk to his father, but it isn't natural for him, if he is sincere, to put into words in every conversation adoration, thanksgiving, repentance, supplications, or other essentials of the perfect prayer. No, he just talks to his father about whatever is on his heart.

Sometimes we might tell God our Father how much we love Him, sometimes we might thank Him for His great gifts to us, and sometimes we might ask Him for things we need. Often, with shame but with a certainty of forgiveness, we must admit to our Father the things we have done wrong. That's a Father-child relationship, a Father-child conversation, but it's a one-sided affair. It's a start, but with the child doing all the talking.

Right here let's see how this might work into a two-way conversation, a talk in which God, the Father, can answer. If the child knows and loves his father and seeks him out to be with him, he wouldn't try to hold his conversation in the middle of Times Square or Grand Central Station, or even the family living room, would he? No, he would find a place where they could be together alone, a quiet place, a secluded place. It would be at a time when the child was sure of having the conversation without interruption. Then under those conditions, the father could speak back to his child, could help him find the answer to his problems, could use the love between the two as a guide to the right choices.

Now, mind you and mind me, prayer is seeking God seeking us constantly. He can speak to us at any time and we can speak to Him, but in the privacy of our dedicated two-way conversations with Him, we can find a fellowship needed for a closer, richer communion with God. As we wash our children's faces we can say, "Lord, keep the heart clean today." As we dig to plant our seed we can say, "Lord, thank You for growing things." As we meet a pitiful soul on a crowded street we can ask, "Lord, show me how to help," but a two-way conversation should be in our special place, at our special time set aside because we need and want to "seek Him seeking us."

The mother of a tiny boy told of his daily conversation with God. She said each night he would go to the window, looking out into the darkness or the starry sky, and then call softly as if to Someone right outside, "God . . . God . . . Hello, God, this is Dickie. I'm going to bed now. I thought you'd like to know it so you can stay close by. Tomorrow we'll be doing lots of important things together. Good night, God. Good night." Simply, trustingly, surely, Dickie was reaching out and holding God by the hand.

You and I can hold His hand too. We can seek Him seeking us, but effort on our part is essential!

Prayer demands far more than words,
  Far more than bended knee,
For prayer is always seeking God
  And knowing He seeks me.

It's sometimes joyous praises sung,
  Sometimes whispered sin,
But always prayer is giving God
  A dwelling place within.

Prayer is listening, quiet and still,
  Prayer is self-denying,
Prayer is bending to God's will;
  Prayer is learned by trying.

CHAPTER III

Tabernacles and Me

"And after six days Jesus taketh with him Peter, and James, and John, and leadeth them up into an high mountain apart by themselves: and he was transfigured before them. And his raiment became shining, exceeding white as snow; so as no fuller on earth can white them. And there appeared unto them Elias with Moses: and they were talking with Jesus. And Peter answered and said to Jesus, Master, it is good for us to be here: and let us make three tabernacles; one for thee, and one for Moses, and one for Elias. For he wist not what to say; for they were sore afraid. And there was a cloud that overshadowed them: and a voice came out of the cloud, saying, This is my beloved Son: hear him. And suddenly, when they had looked round about, they saw no man any more, save Jesus only with themselves."

—MARK 9:2-8 (K.J.V.)

UP TO THIS POINT you and I have been seeking God, trying to be with Him, hoping to find His Holy Spirit living within ourselves. Maybe we are whittling away at the barriers we have thrown up to shut Him out. Maybe we have experienced sudden glimpses of what it's like to be with God. That's entirely possible, you know—to find Him suddenly before us, once we go looking, expecting, asking to find Him in a new, transfigured way. Suddenly, like Peter, we might be able to see the Sonship of Jesus, the Fatherhood of God, and the radiance of the Holy Spirit in a completely different and glorious light.

If this marvelous experience comes to us, how will we receive it, how will it affect us? You and I are like old Peter in so many ways. Will this transfiguration, or new revelation of Jesus, cause us to react as he did?

"Thou art the Christ, the Son of the living God," Peter had said a short time before he climbed that mountain and experienced God.

"I know not this man of whom ye speak," Peter swore just a little while afterwards. Somehow the transfiguration in all its glory didn't change Peter very much, did it? If you and I are blessed with such a sudden glimpse—if it could possibly come to us—will it change us? Will it?

I climbed, one day, to a mountaintop,
To a place apart and high,
And I said, "My Lord is with me here.
I can find Him if I try."

I called Him "Lord" for I had declared,
Like Peter did that day,
"Thou art the Christ, the Son of God,
The Light, the Truth, the Way!"

This I believed, or thought I did.
Yet others could not see
What He is like or how He loves
By knowing Him through me.

As on this hill I climbed with Him,
Transfigured He became!
His face did shine bright as the sun
And I—was clothed in shame.

"It's good to be here," I did cry.
"I'll prove my love for You."
Frantically I tried to think
Of something I could do.

"I'll build a tabernacle to Thy name."
My deeds would draw me near Him.
But then I heard the voice of God:
"This is my Son, oh, hear Him."

The tabernacles I have built!
The shallow life I live,
Checking off my works, my jobs,
Proud of what I give!

And all the time I've missed the point,
Like Peter on that hill.
I've tried to *do* before I've *heard,*
Before I've listened, still.

"This is my Son, please hear Him now."
Listen, listen, you—
And after you have learned His voice
Then *be,* and *know,* and *do.*

Tabernacles that I build! Tabernacles that crumble and fall, all because I did not stop and listen, because I did not seek His will, or know His purpose, or ask His use of my energy, my abilities, my efforts, to build for Him—not a tabernacle, but a life of joyous faith and love and righteousness in the Kingdom of God. Right here, right now, I would like to remind you of those very common tabernacles that I have built. Maybe you build them too. They are not useless, crumbling things in themselves—no, not at all. They become useless to the Master simply because we do not truly hear Him in our frantic, feverish efforts to build.

I suppose the most evident tabernacle of mine is the tabernacle of Service. For example: One whole year I taught little children in the Kindergarten Department of the Sunday school, not because I wanted to, or felt that I belonged there, but because no one else would do it at that time. "I'll work here until you train someone else," I said, "but hurry, please. Twenty-five squirming, exuberant little children will make of me a nervous and an aged woman."

"He loves me too, He loves me too,
I know He loves me too:
If God so loves the little birds
I know He loves me too."

I taught the children to sing and rejoiced when the closing bell rang each Sunday.

"Who wants to be the preacher and pretend to read from God's Book today?" I would ask, and then take a fat little finger and point to the words, "Be ye kind," "Love one another," "Let the children come to me." And all the while I would be wondering how much longer before the parents would come.

Then, one day, toward the end of my year of building my tabernacle of service, I sat in the presence of Death and realized that I had taught five-year-old Mark for the very last time. Mine had been the opportunity to lead that little boy to love and trust Jesus, but it wasn't until too late that I stopped and listened and heard the very words that I had been teaching, "But Jesus said, 'Let the children come to me.' " Then I knew that my task could have been my challenge, my burden could have become my privilege, my tabernacle might have been an important contribution to the Kingdom. These things could have been, but a little boy's funeral is too late to begin to want to show him God.

How about you? Have you checked off your turn at being president of the women of your church, your time to be a circle chairman, your chance to be a Bible teacher? And as you labored, did you listen, and feel, and know that what you were doing was the most important, vital thing in your life as a Christian? If you didn't, if you begrudged the time, if you did not joyously serve, then yours was a tabernacle like mine.

Another tabernacle can be one of Worship. One Sunday in church, I was seated beside an elderly couple, both of whom went sound asleep. Every now and then the man would make a little snorting sound. This would wake up the wife, who would jump and half-whisper, "What's that? What's that?" Then they would both go back to sleep again.

"Why do they bother to come to church at all?" I wondered antagonistically during the pastoral prayer.

"Maybe the high notes of the anthem will stir them up again," I halfway hoped during the offertory. Then I forgot the sleeping Smiths throughout the sermon as I worried lest my Sunday roast might be cooking too much; as I went over in my mind the Bible lesson I was to teach the next day; and as I planned when I might call on the new family in the pew ahead. I was a little indignant each time a snore broke into my thoughts. The last hymn I sang especially loud, for it was time for my sleepy friends to wake up and go home.

"The Smiths slept all through the service," I said after church. And then, suddenly, I admitted to myself, "And so did I. And so did I."

How long has it been since you have sung "Praise God from

whom all blessings flow," and let your heart sing louder than your voice? How often do you begin, "Our Father who art in heaven," and end, "For thine is the kingdom and the power and the glory," a completely different, better person than when you started? How many times on Sunday morning when you enter His house, do you lift up your heart to Him and truly say, "Lord, this little time we have here together, let's make it really count. All that I am, all that I have, all I want to be, is bowed down before Thee now in adoration, in thankfulness, in loving, joyful praise." If you can truly say you do this every Sunday morning, then your worship is always a vital part of your life in His Kingdom—never, like mine that sleepy Sunday, a crumbling tabernacle.

And then there's that tabernacle of Love. How deeply I love those Hungarians, those Chinese, Mexicans, the people everywhere that my missionaries and ministers tell me about. I love them enough to give a sizeable amount of my money —well, fairly sizeable—to help bring them into the Kingdom. I love them whom I have never seen, but I cannot bring myself to like the lonely, unattractive woman who moved across the street from me. She is not a member of any church but I didn't ask her to go with me to my women's meeting because—well—because I had *almost* a carful of my friends and she would not have fitted in. So she stayed at home and I went to my church, and was happy in bringing my gift to Missions for people I love in Jesus' name, people as far away as Budapest, Shanghai, and Tokyo. But when someone read the words, "Go ye" (and "ye" means me) "into all the world" (and "all the world" includes across the street as well as Budapest), my hollow tabernacle of love rose before me.

How big is your love? Is it a ready response to the encompassing love of Christ for all of His children? Or is it a tabernacle that you and I hasten to build because we are Christians and Christians must show their love?

Which shall it be for you and for me who reach up and find Him and for a brief moment see Him in His true light? Which shall it be: a vital part in the Kingdom, or a tabernacle to crumble, meaningless, into dust?

"This is my Son, please hear Him now."
  Listen, listen, you—
And after you have learned His voice
  Then *be,* and *know,* and *do.*

CHAPTER IV

Me? Grow up?

"When they had finished breakfast, Jesus said to Simon Peter 'Simon, son of John, do you love me more than these?' He said to him, 'Yes, Lord; you know that I love you.' He said to him 'Feed my lambs.' A second time he said to him, 'Simon, son of John, do you love me?' He said to him, 'Yes, Lord; you know that I love you.' He said to him, 'Tend my sheep.' He said to him the third time, 'Simon, son of John, do you love me?' Peter was grieved because he said to him the third time, 'Do you love me?' And he said to him, 'Lord, you know everything; you know tha I love you.' Jesus said to him, 'Feed my sheep.'"

—JOHN 21: 15-17 (R.S.V.)

WOULD IT SURPRISE YOU very much to be told that one of the greatest needs that we women have is to grow up? "Oh, dear," we say, "we grew up so terribly long ago, we've almost forgotten what it is like to be young! We've had responsibilities, earned our living, raised our families. Grow up? We did that long ago."

No, we didn't. We didn't really grow up; we just grew older In order to go farther along our way towards finding God completely, you and I, as women, must think seriously about this business of growing up—*up towards Him.*

Paul felt this need to grow up spiritually. He thought it through until he understood it and then, during his whole lifetime, he worked to meet it. He described himself by saying, "When I was a child, I spake as a child, I understood as a child, I thought as a child: but when I became a man, I put away childish things." It took a whole lifetime for Paul to grow up. Much later he felt compelled to help the Corinthian Christians along with their growth, for he plainly told them that it was time for them to grow up and stop being babies. "I fed you with milk, not solid food; for you were not ready for it; and even yet you are not ready." Time to grow up spiritually!

You cannot truthfully say that you have never felt the need for someone stronger than yourself on whom to lean, for someone wiser than yourself from whom to learn, someone to comfort you in sorrow, to soothe you in sickness, and to make life itself worth while. You have felt this need as you have seen yourself wholly inadequate. You've reached out for the one unchanging hope that God's love presents. You accepted the gift, you became a Christian, you joined the church. You were born again. And there you were, a baby in the Kingdom of God. That's as it should be, a new life, a new creature, a new growth—maybe.

Now look at yourself with eyes that are fair, eyes that are completely honest. Have you, have I, continued to grow spiritually a little each day, a little each week, or even a little each year? Have we grown any from that first baby stage when we reach out and take and accept and then hold and do nothing more? Admit it, woman, admit it. We have been living on milk when by this time we should be eating meat.

In our family there were many times when we, as children, had to go to our father and ask for extra spending money. Now this was a thing we never enjoyed, but soon we came to know that an unexpected approach more often brought a hearty laugh and ready response than did a trite, "Please give me some money, Daddy." I remember one method that seemed never to fail, although it was plainly ridiculous to all concerned.

"Oh, Daddy," we would say, with much, much overdone devotion showing, "I love you so much. You are the nicest father in all the world. I wouldn't trade you with anyone anywhere. I love you, I love you, I love you. Please, Daddy, give me a quarter."

This was quite a joke to all of us—such a shallow, empty love. But it's not so funny when we admit the very same approach to God.

On Sunday, Lord, I'll worship Thee,
  I'll sing Thy praises true.
I'll shift the burdens off of me
  And place them all on You.

I'll list my wants, and favors seek,
  But after that we're through.
So please don't bother me all week;
  If need be, I'll call You.

Yes, we women do need to grow up spiritually, and the very first way is in our personal relationship with God. We must put away childish, partial love and grow a love that is whole, complete, unfailing. It's no use to say that love can't grow, that it can't mature, that love is love and there are no varying degrees. That isn't true. Peter's love grew up. He loved Jesus hen he answered that call, "Follow me," but Peter's love isted denial and complete shame before it grew into a mighty ortress, a rock. It became a complete love that answered the Iaster's question sure and true: "Lord, you know that I love ou." I wonder how much too little our love is to look Jesus raight in the eye and say, "Lord, you know that we love ou." To become mature Christians we must grow up in our ove for God.

Then there's another side to "putting away childish things" piritually. We must put this love into practice, make it a owerful force that affects us. When Peter answered, "Lord, ou know that I love you," three times Jesus insisted, "Well hen, Peter, do something about it. Feed my sheep, Peter; eed my lambs, feed my sheep." This kind of "feeding" re-uires a love for God that works *on* and *for* God's other hildren.

We have a spiritual experience and we see a hand stretched ut to us. We feel the nail holes, we understand the Cross, ve admit our inadequacy and we say, "Oh, yes, Lord, we'll ake Your hand. We need it, we want it, we cannot live with-ut it." And then suddenly we realize that clinging to the ther hand of Jesus is the old woman who does our ironing, dirty little Chinese boy, and a leper of India. Don't you see? f we take Him, then we've got to take them. We've got to put his mature love for God, if we can get it, into mature grown-p love for everyone else. Our hearts and souls become so full f love for God that it splashes over on all His other children.

This growing-up process changes our attitudes toward ther people until they seem completely different and we *are* ompletely different. Things that Jesus said are no longer nemory verses to be learned and taught. They are integral arts of our spiritually growing whole. "Love one another" becomes a part of you, and you love so "completely" that the color of skin, cultural background, and economic differences are all unimportant. "Bear ye one another's burdens," and your own grow lighter as you reach out and help to carry someone else's load. "Go and teach," and you go because you cannot stay away, and teach because God's love so fills you that there is more than enough to pour out again and again for someone else to use.

Just as we learn through growth to reach up and say "Father," so we naturally reach out and say, "Brother." We cannot grow upward unless at the same time we grow outward. That changes things a little, doesn't it? One without the other is impossible and we aren't so sure we want to grow outwardly to the extent that we would never have to worry again about how to spend our money, how to use our energies, how to invest our abilities. There would be no real choice on our part if we truly loved God, for suddenly everything we have and all we do would be God-used, God-directed.

Working for the Kingdom in Japan today is a young friend of ours. For his first Christmas in the mission field we wanted to send him something that would make his life more pleasant in that faraway place. We talked it over and finally decided that a gift of money would solve our problem. "He needs so many things," we said; "clothes, books, maybe a short sightseeing trip to refresh his spirits. So we will send him a check with the request that he use it for the thing he really wants and needs the most."

A short time after Christmas we received this note from Japan:

"Dear Friends, Thank you for your very nice gift. Since you gave me the choice I used it for something I wanted and needed more than anything else. I bought a secondhand tape recorder on which I can transcribe good radio programs of organ music. Now I can add this to the worship services that I hold in bombed-out chapels. Thank you for making this vital aid to the glory of God possible."

The thing he wanted most, needed most, was a way to make the experience of worship meaningful to people he had never seen before and might never see again, but people he loved with splash-over love for God. That's a grown-up, meat-eating, sheep-feeding Christian!

A marvelous thing about this growing-up process is that we never finish. Each time we take a step closer to God, our horizon seems to widen and we see new ways in which to grow, new goals to try to reach, new sins that we never before knew we had. Strangely enough each step, each broader scope ahead, leaves us eager and willing to attempt another stretching. We aren't discouraged over what we see before us, only thrilled and thankful over the newness of life brought about by the small progress already made.

Sometimes we feel ashamed to realize that we've slipped back again, and are milk-fed Christians, babies in the Kingdom. Even then, because we have once seen a broader vista, joy and expectancy are not completely lost. We are strangely anxious and ready to try a little meat again. Just a little at a time, just a little more effort in studying His Word, a little more time allotted to conversations with Him, a little more willingness to try His Way, and a new step is made! The meat begins to satisfy.

A crippled children's clinic, in which I've worked, has taught me many things. I suppose patience is one of the most important elements in any kind of progress. The patience of the parents, the patience of the physiotherapists and doctors, and finally the hard-learned patience of the little crippled child himself have all been essential in whatever progress has been made. One child, born with a pitifully twisted foot, was brought time after time. His leg was put in a cast to stretch his foot just a fraction of an inch toward normality. At regular intervals he returned and the cast was torn off, a new one replacing the old, each time forcing the crooked bones a little nearer to being straight.

How like a woman growing spiritually! She begins with a crippled soul that is turned completely away from God. Just a little at a time she twists, she stretches, she pulls, until gradually she turns toward Him. Patiently she seeks, and asks, and tries, until one day she knows that she is turned toward the Light, away from the darkness, with new growth always ahead.

CHAPTER V

Me and My House

"And if you be unwilling to serve the Lord, choose this day whom you will serve . . . but as for me and my house, we will serve the Lord."
—JOSHUA 24:15

ON A COUNTRY ROAD, a few miles away, there is a lovely yard with boxwood and rosebushes, a fence covered with clematis, and huge oak trees spreading their arms in lofty beauty. But something vital is missing. There is no house there, just a chimney left standing, lone and cold. Always that desolate pile of bricks seems to say to me whenever I pass, "Here was a home. Here were windows and doors, rooms and rugs, furniture, food, and here was a family. Now, only a cold, lonely chimney. In one terrible act, fire reached out and destroyed all but this." I think that each time I see a solitary chimney.

And then each time I hear of divorce, suicide, mental breakdowns, personal bankruptcy, or alcoholism, I see that bleak chimney left standing and think, "Here was a home. Here were people loving each other, laughing together, depending on each other, needing each other, building something eternal together. Now, what is left?" I think: If God had been a vital part of each of these homes, would the results have come out the same?

You've always heard that "a man's home is his castle." What is home to a woman? Surely it is her greatest earthly treasure, her fortress of security, her island of devotion. For here the loves of her life are gathered together with bonds that should be, and could be, impossible to break.

Now if a woman truly wants God and seeks Him for herself, she cannot escape a yearning for Him in all realms in which she moves. A woman cannot have God within herself and not seek and express Him in her home. What about you? What about your home?

What kind of home do you have?
Is it a mansion, fine and fair,
Or is it a place where a happy face
Tells of the riches there?

What kind of home do you have?
Just somewhere to sleep, to eat,
Or do strangers find a heart that's kind,
A warmth that makes life sweet?

What kind of home do you have?
Has God come there to stay?
Your treasure then is from within
And will not fade away.

Let us stop for a moment and look at our homes. Let's have a woman-to-woman conversation with ourselves about a woman-to-God relationship. Let's ask ourselves these questions:

Am I completely satisfied with my home? If I could add one thing, what would it be—a new wall-to-wall carpet, a thirty-inch color television set, a baby, or a new feeling of understanding and love?

Do I care enough about my home to be willing to work to try to improve it, to save it?

Would a consciousness of God's presence in my home make a difference? When my mother-in-law comes to visit I act differently. What about God?

What can I do for myself to keep a continuous consciousness of God? Will I devote time to prayer, to Bible study, to learning from the experience of others through worthwhile books? Will I be willing to make my activities God-like rather than God-less?

Once I've found Him, what can I do to help my family find God? Can I prove my own sincerity by letting God make a difference in the way I live? Will I continuously pray for them to find God? Will I overcome my timidity and openly discuss with them what finding God has meant to me and tell them of my yearning for them to know God too?

What can we, as a family, do to continue to grow toward God as we meet life each day? Will we agree to make Him such a vital part of our home that a feeling of His presence dominates our lives? Will we worship together as a family at home? Will we make worship together at church a regular joyous family habit? Can we make the needs of other people a vital concern of our family as we work together to meet those needs?

Now—if I have honestly and conscientiously examined my home in the light of these questions, I've found the way to make it indestructible, not a chimney left standing.

You and I get so mixed up over values. We have a dreadfully difficult time deciding what really matters, don't we? We are so anxious for our children to be happy that we sometimes make the elusive search for happiness their main objective in life. The Little Jack Horners that we nurture have no room for God. To do nothing more than sit in a corner and stuff oneself and then say, "What a good boy am I," develops a pretty weak character, doesn't it? Yet we oftentimes allow such attitudes to grow in our children as we say, "Let him have fun while he can. He will have worries and troubles soon enough." And do we follow the Little Boy Blue pattern also? You know the part about, "Go wake him. Go wake him. Oh, no, not I; for if I do, he's sure to cry." We don't *ever* want him to cry. We want to shield him from all responsibilities, all disappointments, all griefs, until he is aware of nothing but his own comfort and pleasure. Before we know it, his values are all mixed up, and our values have very little purpose.

Why put braces on your little boy's teeth in order to straighten them if his heart's concept of right and wrong is allowed to grow warped and crooked? Why teach my little girl to play a beautiful melody on the piano if her selfish, grasping fingers leave discord and unhappiness wherever she goes? What good will it do your child to know that one plus one equals two if he never learns that *he* plus God equals *everything*?

We do need to evaluate what things we will seek for our children and then set out to help them grow toward such goals for themselves. If our children are convinced that God makes a difference to us, then He will surely become a reality to them. To speak of God in daily conversations will develop a consciousness of His presence in our home. To read and discuss His Word as purposefully and regularly as we do the daily newspaper will emphasize our dependence on God for constant help in meeting the needs of the world about us. To pray naturally together for each other, recognizing our dependence on Him for the blessings He gives, will surely establish security. It will produce a certainty that always there is God and a family who love each member constantly.

Two wedding presents that I received will always help me in my appreciation of what really matters. One was a piece of flat silver in my chosen pattern. A "tomato server" is the name given it in silver catalogues. I suppose it cost ten or twelve dollars. How beautiful it looked in the box when it first arrived. But, do you know something? I've never once in twenty years used it! An expensive present, but of no real value to me at all.

The other gift was a paperback book that cost ten cents. On the day of my wedding, I received a special delivery letter and this little book. The letter said, "My dear Friend, Tomorrow you will begin your home. Begin it with God. The enclosed booklet will help you build a family altar on which the foundations of your home will rest. Tomorrow, when there are many new beginnings, is the best time you'll ever find to start the practice of prayer and Bible reading together." That was the most valuable wedding gift of all that I received. Valuable because, for twenty years, upon a family altar have been poured joys and sorrows, disappointments, troubles, anxieties, and thankfulness to God. It has become a daily necessity in our lives. Things of value? We women know what they are, but sometimes we pretend we don't. We stress *things* and *doing* when, if we would only stop to think, we could plainly see that all that really matters is *God* and *being*. Once we know it for ourselves, show it by our attitudes and actions, then those who fill our hearts and homes will know it too. We can't give our family God. We can't give them to Him, but we can take Him so completely for our own that He will be there and be known without an introduction.

Often we can see no evidence of success resulting from our attempts to make God a reality in our homes, no sign that His way has become *the way* in our family life. We get discouraged because our children seem totally immune to all spiritual endeavors on our part. "We've failed," we say, forgetting completely that God has been our partner in it all and that He has been working too. Suddenly, without warning, those whom we have desired for God show a new understanding or a new quality of His love and we can say with thanksgiving, "Surely the Lord hath done great things!"

On his ninth birthday all our little boy wanted for his present was money. Almost overnight he became aware of the buying power of money, and that was all he considered important for his gift. If everyone would give him silver dollars then he could control the situation and buy exactly what he wanted. So he cleverly spread the word around our very large family of aunts and uncles, who responded without fail. The day was most successful, the yield was great, for eighteen or nineteen shiny silver dollars were stashed away in his secret hiding place.

Early the next day as I began preparations for breakfast, I heard him in his room clinking his dollars together, counting them many times, arranging them neatly in piles. Then the clinking stopped and he called to me, "Mother, come out in the hall a minute, please. I want to tell you something." I put the bacon on "low" and went to the bottom of the steps.

"Mother," he said, hanging over the stair railing, "I've just decided something important."

"You have, son? What is it?"

"You know, before my birthday, I believed that money was the most important thing. Well, now that I have all these dollars, I don't feel any different from the way I felt before. Money doesn't make you happy, does it? Money doesn't really matter." I risked letting the bacon burn a little and asked, "What does really matter?" The dollars clinked once more and then came the answer: "Well, I guess love really matters. Love makes you happy."

No amount of striving on my part could have taught him such a truth, but God working in him made the answer come easily, naturally, surely.

If you could add one thing more to your home, what would it be? Well, love is what really matters, whether you are nine or eighteen or thirty-six or seventy-two. To love God with all thy heart and all thy mind and all thy soul comes first. Thy family and thy neighbor naturally will follow. Then you find yourself and your family possessing what makes you happy, what really and truly matters.

CHAPTER V

My Church—His Body

"Ye have not chosen me, but I have chosen you, and ordained you, that ye should go and bring forth fruit, and that your fruit should remain: that whatsoever ye shall ask of the Father in my name, he may give it you."

—JOHN 15:16 (K.J.V.)

WHY SHOULD IT TAKE A WOMAN SO LONG to discover that she need not seek God alone? Waiting to help her and her family is one never-failing body, the church. She knows the church as an organization to which it is conveniently nice to belong. Where else can one have one's first baby christened and invite all of one's relatives and friends? Where else can one deposit one's children for an hour on Sunday morning to give one's husband a little peace and quiet with his newspaper at home? Where else can one arrange a large church wedding for one's daughter, who certainly deserves the most fashionable kind? And on Easter Sunday, what better place can one find o display and to observe the loveliest of spring hats? Even he desolate numbness that comes at the death of a loved one seems to demand the atmosphere of one's own church. Yes, a woman sees the necessity of church affiliation, but—oh, my goodness—how much she misses as she affiliates!

There are definitely two sides to church membership. There is the getting side and the giving side, both of which are essential in our search for God. Let's look at the getting ide first. That's usually what women look at, isn't it? What's n this thing for me? What can I gain by it? Plenty, woman, plenty.

Suppose, for just a minute, there were no church, no group with which you could identify yourself in your search for God. You've admitted that you had to have Something, that you could not live alone, that God is absolutely necessary for even a halfway peaceful, happy existence. Then what? How can you grow? You have no one to talk to about spiritual hings unless someone else is seeking too. You need human companionship in your striving, for as you fail so often in your Christian way, you taste the bitter dregs of discouragement and you wonder if you alone miss the mark, time and ime again.

Then, one day, your husband, or your child, or someone else you love becomes ill. You pray, and pray, and pray, as earnestly as you possibly can, but you secretly wonder if God s there at all. You walk out in your back yard or to the grocery store and there you see a friend, a neighbor. Before you know it, you are pouring out your heartache to her and saying, "Oh, please pray with me that God will heal, or, at least, cause me to understand." The friend is willing to pra with you, and for reassurance and comfort you and she tc gether dust off the old Bible so long unused on the shelf. Yo find the words, "Where two or three are gathered togethe in my name, there am I in the midst of them." Confiden assurance of God's love flows back into your heart and you ar thankful for the friend. "Ask, and it shall be given you; seel and ye shall find; knock, and it shall be opened unto you, becomes nourishment to your starving faith, as together yo and your neighbor find a blessing in Bible study.

She summons the courage to ask that her sister be invited t study and pray with you. Before you know it, your group ha increased and you find that you are thanking God as wel as asking for His blessings. You find that you pray for th needs of others and then try to help God carry out th prayer. "Be with Mrs. Jones in her sorrow now, dear God, you say, and, after the amen, you hurry to visit Mrs. Jone and take her a pie.

Your group *was* just a few people *needing* God togethe Suddenly, it *is* just a few people *finding* God together an *doing something about it.* That's the church—oh, forgetfu you, forgetful me, that's the church! It's made up of me and women, little children too—all who need God, who nee each other in finding and worshiping Him, who need eac other in becoming effective vessels in His hands.

One more thing is essential to make that group the tru Church: the public acknowledgment that Jesus Christ is th Son of God, that He died in place of sinners, that He ros again, and is the Body of the Church. If a woman is truly seek ing God, it will not take long for her to meet Jesus Chris His Son, and accept Him as her Saviour. Seeking God is th essential beginning to all companionship with Jesus.

Now, don't you see, woman, how much you have to get from the church? Praying together, studying the Bible together, accepting the trained leadership of a loving pastor, helping each other, learning that others are fighting the same weaknesses that we are, making the same mistakes, accepting the same continuous forgiveness, wanting to express God's love in the same ways, all are extra helps toward being with God. All are built together to make the church. You cannot afford to refuse such vital aids in your most important quest.

Jesus put it even more emphatically than that. "You haven't made the choice," He says; "I made it. I chose you. Whether you like it or not, I died for you. Whether you want me to or not, I'm paying the penalty for your sins. Whether you love me or my way or my Church doesn't change the truth that I have already loved you and chosen you and ordained you that you should go and bring forth fruit." That makes it pretty plain, doesn't it?

Now the giving part of church membership also is important because effective ways to express her love for God are absolutely necessary to a growing Christian woman. That's where the "That ye should go and bring forth fruit" part comes in. Jesus makes it plain that fruit-bearing is a necessity in the Christian life. "I am the vine, ye are the branches," He says, and branches must bear fruit. The church makes it possible for me to bear fruit in ways I never dreamed. Through the church I can teach and preach and heal and give necessary material aid throughout the whole wide earth. I can do it through channels established by the church. I can use so many different gifts of God for His honor and His glory because the church puts these gifts to work for Him.

The church shows me new ways in which I can grow, new talents that I never before knew were mine. It gives me an opportunity for group worship, for Bible study, for ways of service that continue to enrich my understanding and love as long as I will accept these unfailing ways to find God. It makes me see that, with honest effort on my part, even I can lead others in the discovery of new meaning in His Word. It might be in teaching little children, or it might be as a circle Bible leader that I get my opportunity; but whatever it is, if I accept, it provides a way to *give* as well as a way to *get*.

At this point, it is wise for you and me to consider the fact that accepting just the jobs that come easy to us will not cause us to experience our greatest potential in Christian growth. It's wonderful to fix flowers for the sanctuary because we love to do it and have that special knack. It is not wonderful, however, to continue to arrange beautiful flowers year in and year out and do nothing more in our church. To do the things we like to do and feel that we do best is fine up to a certain point, but to let our efforts and willingness to serve end here will cause us to grow stagnant and superficial.

If I am going to serve wholeheartedly in my church, it isn't up to me to say, "I'll serve only in ways that come easy to me or in ways that I enjoy," and then stop and say, "Lord, that's all I want to do." You can't do that with God. He says, "Follow me," and you and I must go wherever He takes us, not where we want to go.

Bible study is a good (or bad) example of this leading. To every Christian woman, at some time or other, Jesus says, "Come and *get* by studying my Word, and then come and *give* by sharing it with others." Probably the weakest point in most of our churches today is the unwillingness of Christian women (and men) to attempt Bible study for themselves and others. Maybe you and I can find some way to see this as a challenging opportunity rather than a frightening "turn" to take. Let's take the dreadful dilemma of having to teach a Bible lesson to women. Let's look plainly at two people before we start, ourselves and the woman we teach.

First, me or you. Have you ever done anything worth while or successful or good that did not take time, effort, and a keen desire to do that thing well? Do you often make a good cake when you don't half try? Or a dress? Have you ever made one to fit when you began with the idea, "Oh, well, it will look terrible no matter what I do, so I won't try very hard"? No, you haven't. It is only when you've patiently, honestly, caringly tried that you've been satisfied with the results. And you cannot whip up a satisfying Bible lesson, either, without being willing to put yourself out.

Then there is another thing about you and me that we must see as an essential to a good Bible study. We must admit the need of God's Holy Spirit. Of course you cannot teach a meaningful Bible lesson purely on your own, but with God's help that He gives every time you ask it, His Holy Spirit can strengthen you, encourage you, and lead you as you earnestly try to find the meaning of His Holy Word.

Now, let's look at that woman we shall try to teach. One great reason for failure in teaching women is that sometimes we go on the assumption that each woman there is sitting before us like an empty cup just waiting to be filled, that she is anxious to hear and will remember anything and everything we say or read. Now that just isn't true and you know it. She is not hanging on your every word. She does not have an eagerness for anything you happen to say or read. Quite often she has much besides you on her mind, and it takes a little jarring sometimes to bring her back to you and what you teach.

Then another great reason for failure is that we go to the other extreme. We decide that this woman just isn't going to listen, no matter what we say, so it really doesn't make any difference if we don't say anything. That isn't true either. Every person you know is seeking, seeking something, and if you or I have even a fifteen-minute opportunity to help her find that something, what a thrilling, exciting challenge Bible-sharing can become! Multiply the fifteen minutes by the number of women in your group and see how much time God could be using you as a chosen vessel.

A willingness to pray and a willingness to work are two essentials to good Bible teaching. "Wait," you say, "other things are necessary. Personality, poise, self-assurance, ability to speak—these are necessary." They do help, but they will come when you really try the other two things. Remember Moses who couldn't speak? There wasn't anything wrong with his poise or self-assurance when he came down from the mountain where he had been with God. And there will not be anything lacking in you and me if we first go up on the mountain and then do our very, very best.

There is just one other thing I'd like to remind us of in this getting ready to teach. To get anywhere, to reach any woman, you and I must care about that woman. We must love her enough not to say, "Oh, she's so worldly and sinful and disinterested that there is nothing I can say to reach her." No, we must love her enough to say, "God, that lost child of yours needs You. Help me to love her enough to make her see Your love for her."

Such an approach could be used for any responsibility we take on in the church. Whether it be pastor's aid, kindergarten superintendent, circle chairman, or Bible teacher, prayer and willingness to work can make them all possible if we really want God.

You and I can't afford to leave out the church in our search for God. It provides us with worship, the food a searching soul craves. It provides us with fellowship, the feeling of *togetherness* in so exciting an adventure. It provides us with leadership, as a pastor or a teacher helps to lead us into light. It provides us with objectives that channel energies and abilities into lasting, vital tools of God. It provides us with a Saviour who loved us enough to be willing to suffer the painful, shameful death of the cross in order that we might never have to die.

Live without the church? I suppose it is possible, for ever so many unhappy people do. But live *meaningfully* without the church? I would hate to have to try it, for I need everything it offers to help me find God. *Don't you?*

O God, we can understand the protective love of a shepherd for his sheep and we thank You that You have that love for us. We have learned the self-denying love that a father has for his child and we thank You that You love us that way. Great sovereigns have proved to us the kind of love that a noble king has for his lowest subject and we are grateful that You care for us like that. But the redemptive love of a Saviour hanging on a cross in our place is a love that we shall never be able to comprehend or deserve or imitate completely. O God, we thank You for that kind of love. To be a member of His Body, the Church, is truly the greatest of all our blessings. Help us to remember it now, tomorrow, and always. In His name.

Amen.

CHAPTER VII

My Community—where I take Him

JUST AS A WOMAN cannot find God by seeking Him on Sunday and leaving Him completely out of her life the other six days of the week, neither can she use Him in church and discard Him in her social and civic relationships. Finding God is a complete undertaking, a complete commitment, a complete acceptance. A woman cannot pigeonhole her finding God into church activities, church associations; for once she possesses Him, then He possesses her, and no area of her life can shut Him out. He permeates, infuses, takes over all realms in which she moves. And here, my sister, comes the most difficult part in being a Christian.

It's fairly easy to sing praises together in the church, to glow with good-deed-doing through service in the church, to find a certain measure of sincerity in our "love my church" attitudes, but once God begins to take over our social, civic, and economic relations, then—well, we aren't quite ready to go all the way. After all, we have our circle of dear, dear friends who expect certain social habits and standards from us. Who are we to be so sanctimonious and holy that we suddenly say, "No, that's not the way a woman who has found God expresses her love for Him; that's not the Christlike way"? Why, these friends we've known and counted so important for such a long time would be offended. They would laugh at our prim decision, would probably not bother to invite us next time.

And to be a Christian in our civic responsibilities . . . It just wouldn't be practical! Taxes now are far too high. Anything done to help the underprivileged, the unfortunate in our community, would certainly be expensive. In our political relationships we must continue to support "the party." After all, who are we to be different from our fathers and grandfathers who always voted for the party? Besides, there are certain favors that are due us for such loyalty—and we intend to get them.

To take the principles of Jesus into our economic planning —why, that would be foolish too. That would be impractical. To pay a late day-worker for an hour she must miss because of a sick child at home, to return the too much change to the checker at the supermarket when things are as high as they are, to give my old coat to the ironing woman instead of making her work out the pay for it, why, these things involve money and I need all I can get.

How do you suppose Jesus feels when He sees inside of you and me who have reached out to accept Him as Lord and Saviour? He must feel as He did that day on the hill outside Jerusalem when He said, "O Jerusalem, Jerusalem . . . how often would I have gathered thy children together, even as a hen gathereth her chickens under her wings, and ye would not!"

Think it through, woman, think it through. Have you, have I, any right at all to expect to have God if we won't let Him have us? A halfway Christian can be far more harmful to the Kingdom than a no-way Christian. She not only is blocking off herself from God, she is also blocking off other people, who say, "If she's a Christian, I don't want to be one," or "She's a Christian and she does certain questionable things, so I guess it's all right for me to do them too."

In a questionnaire recently given to teen-agers in our community, some startling answers were noted. To the question, "What is your greatest problem as a young person?" came this answer in many different forms: "My greatest problem? It is the behavior of adults." The behavior of Christian adults in a Christian community of a Christian nation is admittedly the greatest problem of some honest-thinking teen-agers. They don't know what to count on, what to believe in, when they see supposedly Christian men and women using God just on Sunday.

"Social drinking as we do it," said a friend of mine, "has no harm in it. None of us ever overindulge; at least, we haven't yet. Why, I see nothing wrong in it for a Christian. Besides, over half of the elders in my church drink. Why shouldn't I?" No harm in it? How far can a woman see? What woman takes her first drink with the intention of becoming an alcoholic? Distressing, startling statistics prove that each year the number of women alcoholics is increasing, that one of the greatest factors in broken homes is alcoholism, that loss of young life and old life from traffic accidents is increasing in a frightening way because of "driving while intoxicated." Can you be absolutely sure, O Christian woman, that there will be "no harm" in the way your boy or your girl will react to social drinking learned from you?

Wise old Paul, in writing to the Corinthians, warned you and me of just such a "no harm" attitude. "Take heed," he says, "lest by any means this liberty of yours [meaning the eating of sacrificial meat] become a stumblingblock to them that are weak. . . . Wherefore, if meat make my brother to offend, I will eat no flesh while the world standeth, lest I make my brother to offend." Can you, having found God, afford to become a stumbling block?

There are other social pitfalls that you and I must avoid in order to express God completely in our everyday living. Extravagance in "keeping up with the Joneses" can lead our children up a false-sense-of-values avenue. Insincerity and hypocrisy in choosing and keeping our friends can cause shallow, meaningless relationships of no real value to true companionship. Using friendship as a steppingstone to commercial gain or as an entree to a more desired social group can make dishonesty become second nature to us. Honest, sincere, unselfish love is what we must feel for God's other children or we have not truly found God.

This kind of love carries over into our civic and economic associations also. One cannot possibly be separated from the other. Civic betterment in any community is somewhat dependent upon the economic level of its society. To express love throughout a community, a woman must see the proper relationship of possessions to civic responsibility. Possessions entail far more than money, for understanding, energy, ability, are essential in any undertaking to help one's neighbor. But money comes in, too, just as it does in the church.

Recently, a most interesting experiment was carried out in our community. In his budget message, the city manager of our town stated: "We have a permanent planning commission composed of the best qualified citizens available to plan continuously for our physical needs. We spend a big part of each council meeting discussing physical requirements of the community. Nowhere does there seem to be a corresponding interest in the human needs."

He recommended that a Commission on Human Values composed of interested citizens be appointed to study this field. The City Council accepted the challenge, and for one whole year over two hundred citizens from all walks of life worked together to understand the human needs in our community. Studying such phases of community life as Welfare Services, Court Procedures, Health Programs, Prison Administration, Education for Non-normal Children, Recreation Guidance, Teen-age Problems, and Law Enforcement, the Commission set as its objective "the formulation of a program not for the purpose of spending money, but as a means of aiding each citizen to improve mentally, physically, and spiritually." Invaluable recommendations to City Council were the tangible results of this adventure in citizenship that will bear fruit into the future. Perhaps the greatest benefit was an *awareness* of the needs of others that resulted from the study. Surely God can take such efforts of His children and use them to His honor and glory.

But we must be willing to put out the efforts, to care

enough to feel responsible for our neighbor. When someone asked Jesus, "Who is my neighbor?" the answer was clear: "Anyone who needs your help—he is your neighbor." When you and I become truly aware of our neighbor as a result of our awareness of God, then there is no end to our neighborhood, no finish to helping others, and never, never, never again a feeling of being alone or without purpose.

I suppose now is the time for you and me to consider material possessions, what belongs to God and what belongs to us. Next to taking God into one's social life, this business of taking God into one's pocketbook is the most difficult step for a Christian to make. I don't know why it should be. Goodness knows, we have only to look at all of the blessings God heaps upon us and know that through no efforts or deserving on our part do such things come. What have I done to warrant the brightness of day or the blessedness of fresh air and cool water? Why should I have heaped upon me a family's love, friendship I can rely upon, and most wonderful of all, a Saviour who died in my place? Certainly if I can ever come to understand that these great gifts of God are not due me, not owed me, not rightfully mine because of anything I have done, but are mine as a gift of God, then I could know that such is the case with the dollars in my bank account.

Once a woman understands that nothing really belongs completely to her except God's unfailing love, and that such love is in itself His greatest gift, then among her possessions money will be seen in proper perspective. Since all is God-given, all becomes God-directed, God-used. To me, Dr. Stanley Jones' answer to the question, "What of my material wealth should be set aside for God to use?" is the best I've ever heard. Dr. Jones reminds us that after all our God-given possessions have been dedicated to Him, we may use for ourselves only "as much of it as will make us more physically, mentally, and spiritually fit for the purposes of the Kingdom of God." That's a pretty good rule to follow, isn't it? The terrific decision regarding the new coat, the vacation plans, the new rug for the living room, will not be quite so terrific with such a guiding factor. The question is, woman who wants God, are you willing to adopt such a rule?

How much your church pledge should be, how much you can give to the Community Chest, to what extent you should try to take care of your old maid aunt, all will assume their relative importance once you have sought and found. To give in secret to someone near you who desperately needs help can become a joyous blessing to you. Such a "cup of cold water" in Jesus' name starts out to enrich someone else's life and ends up enriching yours. Try it, woman, and see. Try it as your love enlarges to include giving, and doing, and being in a community in ways that will truly glorify God.

CHAPTER VIII

God's Interruptions

A WOMAN WANTS GOD. She wants Him enough to be willing to serve Him—in her own time, after her own choosing, according to her own planning. And it takes a bit of planning for a busy woman-child of God to get all of life dealt with. She must be, by all modern standards, an executive who makes and keeps a schedule; who manages wisely the ever-shrinking dollars in her trust; who, authoritatively, settles disputes with a wisdom greater than Solomon the king.

She must be a cook, chauffeur, seamstress, gardener, sportswoman, solicitor, a member of the Red Cross, Cancer, Mental Health, Tuberculosis, Heart, and Et Cetera Associations. She is expected to march when the mothers march, to camp out with the Cubs, to bake with the Brownies, to attend music recitals, PTA programs, and never miss a day of being informed on world affairs. She must know how to make a cheap home permanent look like a twenty-dollar one, to make witch's hats, pirate's swords, angel wings, a triangular flower arrangement or a Hogarth Curve. She must be continually learning new ways to solve new problems as she discovers such basic truths as that changing a baby's diapers is much, much easier than changing a teen-ager's mind. She must strive never to lose her self-control, figure, temper, teeth, good standing with her in-laws, direction booklets that come with electrical appliances, or the once-a-week cleaning woman in her life. Oh, yes, a woman must be an executive of the highest order if she is to fulfill her expected functions in modern society.

To meet the demands made upon her today, woman must surely plan ahead. She must have a schedule, make lists, and meet deadlines with calm precision. Yet with all this efficiency expected as a matter of course, woman must continually find herself dealing with the unexpected.

I don't suppose there is anything that a busy woman has any more of than she does interruptions. These, in the face of a well-planned schedule, can be terribly irritating, can't they? While busily working out some mental problem recently, I was interrupted twice within two minutes with these queries: "Mother, who invented the zipper?" and "What makes chigger bites itch?" Such questions all day long can make a busy woman's life pretty hectic, can't they?

And even at night, we cannot be too sure of uninterrupted sleep. So often in the middle of the night I awake suddenly to realize that someone is calling me. I find myself stumbling through the dark to my little boy's room to hear, "Mother, I'm having bad dreams." And, like you do, I crawl in bed with him to hold him close until he is no longer afraid and goes happily back to sleep. And I—I am awake until dawn.

You can think of the days when you've planned to clean the basement and ended up by talking over the telephone ten times, leaving a bigger mess than ever downstairs. You can remember the cakes you've ruined because of a persistent magazine salesman at the front door. And, if you are truly honest, you will admit the times you've ended the day ashamed of the way you have yelled at the children the dozenth time they interrupted your thinking or schedule with their questions and requests.

Oh, yes, we have our interruptions, you and I, and often we let them get the best of us. We fail to realize that sometimes—sometimes—they are the only way God has of breaking into what we have planned, what we would like to do, what we think is important.

Let's look back at old Peter for a minute.

"Now Peter and John were going up to the temple at the hour of prayer, the ninth hour. And a man lame from birth was being carried, whom they laid daily at that gate of the temple which is called Beautiful to ask alms of those who entered the temple. Seeing Peter and John about to go into the temple, he asked for alms. And Peter directed his gaze at him, with John, and said, 'Look at us.' And he fixed his attention upon them, expecting to receive something from them. But Peter said, 'I have no silver and gold, but I give you what I have; in the name of Jesus Christ of Nazareth, walk.' And he took him by the right hand and raised him up; and immediately his feet and ankles were made strong And leaping up he stood and walked and entered the temple with them, walking and leaping and praising God And all the people saw him walking and praising God.'

This is the same Peter who denied his Lord, but it's a new Peter who has experienced the Resurrection. He has become the Rock on which so much depended. Now, Peter was a very busy man. You'll agree to that. Much of the responsibility o that first Christian church was upon his shoulders. I'm sure that when he went to bed at night he was tired. Every minute of his day was filled with doing good things, worth-while things. I imagine that Peter had to push and push hard to ge everything in. To find a time to go to the Temple to pray was hard to do, but he found that time. I can see him wit John, hurrying, as they approached the Temple at the nint hour. And then, just as he got to the gate and started in, he met his interruption, a lame man asking alms.

I wonder if Peter felt as I do sometimes when someone breaks into my plans, my good, worth-while plans. I resent their breaking in, and sometimes I even refuse to be interrupted. Do you? Well, Peter didn't. He stopped, he listened he responded, and before he knew it that walking, skipping jumping, dancing, completely healed man had paved the way for one of the greatest sermons Peter ever preached, so great that about five thousand men believed in the Lord Jesu Christ.

That was one of God's interruptions. That was the way God got His work done that day. And do you know something? Peter didn't get to say his prayers as he had planned but Peter walked with God and felt Him very near.

Do you see what I'm trying to open my eyes and your eyes

to? It's just this. Sometimes the only way God can use us is to interrupt us. If we've filled our day so full of good things, and bad things, that there's no time left to be used of God, then He must interrupt us. If we've made our plans, good plans or bad plans, then the only way God can get in His plan is to interrupt us. And you and I aren't capable of judging always just what things God would have done each day.

Maybe the magazine salesman has never experienced the fullness of God's love and your loving kindness would strengthen him. Maybe one of the ten telephone calls is from a lonely friend who could find in you far more of a treasure than silver and gold. Maybe my attitude toward my child's endless questioning could pave the way for trust and understanding later on when she is desperately in need of the right answers and the right understanding. Maybe my soul is hungry for the meditation time that wakeful hours provide when I cannot go back to sleep after my little boy's bad dreams. Maybe that's God's way of making me find time to seek Him seeking me.

You see now what I mean, don't you? Who are we, you and I, to decide that this, this will be my day, and refuse the interruptions that God must send to make it His day?

> "Busy day, busy day, busy, busy, busy day.
> Wash the clothes, sweep the floor,
> Iron the clothes, and sweep some more—
> Busy, busy, busy day.
> No time to make dessert!"

These aren't the exact words of the little jingle that comes to me so often from a television program, but they have the same meaning. Each time I hear this advertising gimmick designed to make me rush to the store to buy prepared puddings for dessert, I find myself thinking, "How sad, how true!"

Women today are faced with such a dilemma. And it goes far deeper than just not having time to make a pie or bake a cake. It goes deeper. Then I find myself chanting:

> "Busy day, busy day, busy, busy, busy day.
> Plan the meals, shop in town,
> Meetings, meetings all around—
> Busy, busy, busy day.
> No time to hear what God would say."

Would it change the hectic push of our days any at all if you and I could get up each morning with this thought in mind: "Today will be filled with interruptions and some of them might just happen to be God's way of getting His work done by me. They might be His way of putting into my life a hidden treasure that He wants me to receive. Will I be willing, like Peter, to take advantage of this day and whatever God will send? Maybe not five thousand will be my result, but maybe two or three or maybe just one—me—will be added to the Kingdom."

Let us pray.

O God, interrupt us today in our earthly, worldly, unimportant plannings. Make us aware that not always are our plans Your plans. Help us to see opportunities in interruptions and to use them for Thy honor and Thy glory.
Amen.

CHAPTER IX

A Hatful of Joy

"These things have I spoken unto you, that my joy might remain in you, and that your joy might be full."

—JOHN 15:11 (K.J.V.)

JOY! A BUBBLING-OVER OF GLADNESS that's for you and for me. Joy, that fills our beings if we have truly found God! Joy, that's mine, that's yours! But—is it? Is it?

Some days my joy isn't so very full; is yours? Some days, because I refuse to remember, I forget all the things that could make my joy full. I forget all about the love that Jesus pours out upon us, forget that He said, "Ye have not chosen me, but I have chosen you." Now, really, can you think of anything more worthy of joy than to know that you belong to Jesus Christ, the Son of the Living God?—that you are His because He chose you to be His to the point of laying down His life in your place? You are His!

Some days I forget that He said, "Lo, I am with you alway," reminding me that I need never be afraid or alone again. And I forget something else that could bring me such joy. Jesus needs me. He can use me. He has something important for me to do, something that no other child of His can do in just the same way. Think about it, woman. He needs you in a place that no one else can fill. That's the exciting, thrilling part of being a Christian—only, you and I forget it, and our joy is not full.

O sister of mine, if you and I aren't careful, in our quest to find God we will become so concerned with striving that we will miss the power that comes from a fullness of joy. You see, the joy is ours to be used if we will just become aware of the marvelous blessings of our lives. We take so many things for granted that, unconsciously, *we look to see what's missing and overlook what's there.* Our little boy wanted a rifle one Christmas, and because he didn't get it, he saw none of his other gifts. He looked only for the thing not there. And his joy was not at all "full."

You and I do that in our search for God, and we become ineffectual Christians without the power that a fullness of joy inevitably brings. When this joy is lacking, the power is curtailed; and a watered-down Christianity without the force of joy can never effectively win others to the Kingdom. You and I have accepted the gift, now let's find the fullness of joy that generates the power to respond to the gift.

Honestly, woman, I truly believe that the secret of finding

joy is simply remembering—remembering blessings. Remembering that God made you, and that He then bought you back again because He loves you, will nudge the joy hidden in your heart a little more to the front. Remembering that relying on yourself you can do nothing, but that relying on Him you can do "all things," will activate the joy a little more.

But if remembering all of these greatest gifts fails to overflow your joyful cup, then take a look at your Sunday hat and remember the Bredoskins.

I'll never forget the first time I saw the Bredoskins. On a freezing day in November, they came timidly into our church. They seemed to be only half sure that someone wouldn't turn them back into the cold as they haltingly followed the usher down the aisle.

Mama Bredoskin was seated at one end of the short side pew, Papa at the other end, and the two little boys were still and silent in between. Papa's face was marked with heavy lines of suffering, but his eyes were friendly and even twinkled back when anyone smiled at him. The little boys, in their homemade Sunday suits, seemed almost too solemn and too wise.

And Mama? With her head tied securely in a large silk scarf, she sat motionless staring straight ahead. Her face did not tell as much as Papa's, but every now and then I noticed a gesture that tugged at my heart. She would raise one hand and quickly wipe her eyes just as a child might do who was afraid she would cry. Her clothes, like Papa's, were American, but of flimsy material characteristic of our bargain basements. Only her head scarf marked her as foreigner to anyone who looked over the hatted heads of the women in our congregation.

In front of Mama Bredoskin sat Alice Dalton in her Hattie Carnegie hat from New York. Across the aisle sat Annette Andrews who runs a hat shop and creates her own models. Every woman in the church wore some kind of a hat—old or new, unbecoming or flattering, cheap or expensive, but, nevertheless, hats. And here sat Mrs. Bredoskin with her bright-colored scarf tied under her chin.

After the benediction, I tried to welcome them and discovered that they understood almost no English at all. They continued to come each Sunday, though, and the members of our church tried in every way they could to help the Bredoskins become adjusted. After all, they had chosen us and were ours to do something about whether we could speak their language or not. They understood smiles, handshakes, a genuine welcome, and that seemed to be sufficient for the time being.

We were able to piece together a little information about our newest church family. They were "D.P.'s"—a name Mama hated with a vengeance, for evidently someone had hurled it at them in an unkind way. As Displaced Persons, they were allowed into the United States under the sponsorship of a farmer who lived several miles out of town. Papa had never been a farmer, but when the opportunity came to get to America by claiming to be one, he took it. You would have, too, if you had been pushed all over Europe as they had. They had first been run out of Czechoslovakia by the Germans and then forced out of the Ukraine by the Russians.

When Papa turned out to be such a failure at farming, his sponsor helped him get a job at a furniture plant. Here he fitted in better, for during the war he had worked in a Russian munitions factory which the allies destroyed along with three fingers of Papa's right hand. His appreciation of his chance to begin over again in America gave me an uncomfortable feeling of shame.

As the weeks passed, the Bredoskins became more a part of our church. Once, when I sat on the row in front of them, I heard Mama humming the Doxology lustily. She still didn't know the words, but she was catching on to the tune. The Sunday school superintendent reported the receipt of a crumpled envelope containing four one-dollar bills and a note, "We gif one dola to Church." It was signed Ivan, Dousa, Tola, Ladime Bredoskin. Oh, yes, the Bredoskins were catching on!

At every meeting of the women of our church somehow or other we would get on the subject of a hat for Mrs. Bredoskin. Several well-meaning ladies had hats they wanted to give her but couldn't quite get up the nerve. Would she be offended? Would she feel that the silk scarf stood for something we did not welcome in our church? Always we decided against giving her one. Mama should never be made to feel that we had ever noticed that she didn't have a hat, that she wasn't exactly like the rest of us.

One Saturday, early in April, a neighbor of the Bredoskins called me on the telephone.

"Mrs. Bredoskin wants you to come to her house," she said.

"Is she sick?" I asked.

"No, she wants you to do something for her. I'm not sure what, but I think it's something about her head."

"Her head? Has she hurt it some way?"

"No, she's all right. But she keeps pointing to her head and saying things I can't understand. I'm afraid she wants you to give her a home permanent."

"Heaven forbid!" I had a mental picture of Mama's thick black hair that was waist-length. "I hope you are wrong, but tell her I'll come," I said.

When I reached their little house, all four were waiting, so excited that it took at least five minutes for me to calm Papa into my kind of English. At last he got through to me. He seized a mail order catalogue, and pointed to a page showing the very best buys in ladies' hats.

"Hats," I said, still completely in the dark.

"Okay," rejoiced Papa. "You buy Mama hat, I pay," and he dug his hand deep in his pockets to bring out proof that he could.

"Okay," I happily agreed, and I found myself setting out with Mama, Papa, Tola, and Ladime to do the thing most important in all of their lives at the moment—to buy Mama an American hat! And this was no easy task.

In the first place, Papa's money must be adequate, and three dollars didn't give us much choice. Then, Mama's long hair presented another problem. However, these were not my greatest concern. When I found a hat that we could afford, and that would fit, Mama wouldn't like it. If she did, then Papa wouldn't like it, and soon Ladime and Tola even had their say in the matter. We visited every cheap hat bar in the town, throwing each one into complete, chaotic confusion, and Mama still wasn't satisfied.

"Please," she finally said, "excuse, please. Lady, church, Sunday. I sit here. She sit—one, two, three rows front. Lady hat—good, okay." Frantically I tried to remember who sat where at church the Sunday before and what kind of hats they wore.

"Do you mean Mrs. Dalton, the lady with flowers all over her hat?" I asked.

Mama beamed. That was exactly whom she meant. The hat she was describing had cost thirty-five dollars if it cost a cent. Mrs. Bredoskin was no fool. She had picked out the best hat in church.

I was desperate. How could I possibly keep from disappointing Mama who wanted a creation for two ninety-eight? Suddenly, I realized the answer. Mama wanted flowers, most of all she wanted flowers.

"You wait here," I acted out. "I come back—five minutes." There was nothing else for them to do but agree. The four of them stood unhappily in the aisle between Ladies' Hats and Ladies' Underwear while I dashed to the ten cent store next door and made my purchase. For two dollars and a half I bought a powerful lot of artificial flowers.

Hopefully I raced back and searched out the last hat that I had found able to cover Mama's head and hair. I put it on her, and before she could object to it again, I simply smothered it in flowers. And do you know something? It really did remind you of Alice Dalton's treasure!

"How much cost?" doubted Papa.

"Flowers, one dollar," I compromised. "Hat, one dollar ninety-eight cents. Sew flowers to stay."

"Okay," said Mama.

"Okay," said Papa, and his eyes spoke happiness complete.

"Okay," echoed Ladime and Tola, who somehow understood that the day was made.

When the last flower was securely fastened, Mama put on the hat, looked long at herself in the mirror, and then, turning to me with a light upon her face I had never seen before, she said, "Thank you. Now, no more D.P. Now American!" She had attained a joy that she had come halfway around the world to find!

I went home and got down my best hat. It wasn't shabby or out of style to me any more. It was beautiful! And as I looked, I saw things I'd never seen before, things that went along with that piece of blue felt—a way of life, a priceless treasure, a glorious heritage.

Suddenly I found myself saying, "Thank You, oh, thank You, God." And do you know what? I was down on my knees.

A hatful of joy! That's what remembering brings. And we need to remember it all over and over again.

Look at yourself in the mirror, and say to yourself, just as surely, as triumphantly as Mama Bredoskin, "Now, no more unhappy woman, now child of God!"

CHAPTER X

Adventure begun

Straight to the house I built for him
  The happy bluebird goes.
How does he find it waiting there?
  Who tells him all he knows?

How does my garden know to bloom
  In season, all year through?
The flowers grow and bud in turn.
  Who tells them what to do?

My baby nestles at my breast.
  She knows her mother well.
How can she feel the love I hold?
  Who teaches her to tell?

All but a woman or a man
  Seem sure that God is nigh.
The bluebird, flowers, and my child
  Can trust Him, why can't I?

HAS THE TIME FINALLY COME for you and me to get down on our knees? Surely by now we have admitted that we lack something vital. Maybe we just need a beginning. There's no better place to begin than on our knees. Maybe we need a learned prayer to push us off. Surely we're too big for the "Now I lay me" one. And the other, the Lord's Prayer? Well, it's a pretty costly one to pray sincerely.

You know why it's costly, don't you? Because there are so many things you and I must give up before we can pray it. We will have to give up prejudice and racial pride on the very first words, "*Our Father,*" casting in our lots with all the peoples of the earth. We will have to give up all halfway commitment when we say, "*Hallowed be thy name.*" And we must pay dearly for the next part, for to say, "*Thy will,*" giving up "my will" gladly, wholeheartedly, sincerely—well, that's going all the way with Him. "*Daily bread*" means necessities, things that we actually need to glorify Him more fully. 'Twill be hard to sneak in so many things we have counted important. Asking for forgiveness, promising to *forgive,* wipes out all grudges, jealousies, holding back of love, and to do that, sister, we have to admit a powerful lot of faults and weaknesses. "*Keep us out of trouble, Lord,*" well, that's not so hard to ask once we've truly prayed the other, but be sure you mean it, woman, before you say it.

If you can get that far, kneeling there crying out to God—not just with words, but with the truth—then you've finally reached acceptance of what you've found in seeking God. Once we do this, then the last part of the prayer, *"For thine is the kingdom, and the power, and the glory, for ever,"* becomes a new-found blessing. You see, when we get right down to accepting the joy that should be ours, then this last part has a double meaning. All these things that belong to God are ours too. "For mine is the Kingdom." I am God's and He is mine and we build together. And "the power"? Certainly the Power is mine, because with God using me to do His work we are a mighty, triumphant, powerful force that nothing can stop. And "glory"? Glory is joy in its fullest form, forever and ever, Amen!

How did you come out of it, my sister? How did that time

on your knees leave you? Well, the Bible is the next step if you want it written down in one-two-three form. You have a Bible, haven't you? Or one of the children has? Someone, an aunt, a grandmother, or a friend, surely gave one to someone in your family for a birthday or graduation or Christmas. Get it out, woman, get it out. Let it fall open just about in the middle and there you'll find Psalms. Find the Twenty-third Psalm and I'll do it too. We are off our knees by now, but in truth our hearts still kneel at His Throne waiting, waiting, waiting.

> *"The Lord is my shepherd; I shall not want."*

Oh, sister, sister, did you read it? Did you fully understand it? Just exactly what you and I started out to find is here, here. We wanted God. We needed something so terribly, and if we have let ourselves accept Him we've found the answer to that need. We can call Him a Shepherd who leads us, or a Father who stays with us, or a Saviour who died for us, or the Holy Spirit who moves in us. Whatever we call Him, we know now He is the Answer.

> *"He maketh me to lie down in green pastures: he leadeth me beside the still waters."*

I was so tired of not knowing which direction to take, so weary with endless struggles to find a relaxed and peaceful heart, and now He can take over. He can and He will feed me, a sheep of His beloved Flock. Relaxed, undisturbed sleep is mine now, for "still waters" can untangle nerves when He leads me there.

> *"He restoreth my soul: he leadeth me in the paths of righteousness for his name's sake."*

How badly my soul needeth restoring! Did yours? My soul had found no answer for so long that it was almost hidden and lost to me. But He made it whole again, has given it a voice that speaks loud and clear, has furnished it a purpose in being. The paths of righteousness won't always be easy, I know, but He will be leading me and that's all I need to be used for His Honor and His Glory.

> *"Yea, though I walk through the valley of the shadow of death, I will fear no evil: for thou art with me; thy rod and thy staff they comfort me."*

Oh, the blessed relief and assurance that brings! So many times I've forced fears of death out of my mind, but always they pricked at the peace of my soul. Now, I need never to fear again. Death itself won't touch me or those I love who believe. Only its shadow will fall and I will remember something I learned as a little girl—shadows cannot hurt or destroy. As long as He is with me and I can stay within reach of His staff, His rod, His hand, death will be merely as passing through a shadowy valley into brightness of the everlasting heights.

> *"Thou preparest a table before me in the presence of mine enemies: thou anointest my head with oil; my cup runneth over."*

As I follow Him there will be enemies, His enemies and mine. Not because I won't forgive them are they enemies, but because they oppose His way. He will take care of my needs in the presence of evil. I can trust Him for physical strength to do His will. I can look to Him for healing and comfort should I suffer pain in my assignments from Him. With it all will be a fullness of life that is so complete I cannot ask for more.

> *"Surely goodness and mercy shall follow me all the days of my life: and I will dwell in the house of the Lord for ever."*

Blessed, blessed assurance of eternity with Him! What more can I hope for? What else really matters?

Now, down on our knees again, sister, on our knees to listen. Work He has for me to do—work that no one else can do in the same special way—is too important to begin without His guidance. Maybe I won't hear anything too exact, too special this first time. Maybe I'll just feel His Presence. It may be that I'll find it necessary to go back to my busy, busy day before I'm sure what He wants me to do. But as I go I'll still be listening, waiting, responding. For He and I will walk together today.

Oh, sister, sister, sister! You've wanted Him. You've searched for Him. Possibly now you have found Him. The next step is the exciting, thrilling challenge that makes all the difference in living. Now—use Him and let Him use you.

Quoted Material

(IN ORDER OF APPEARANCE)

CHAPTER II • *To Seek Him Seeking Me*

Luke 11:9-10. This and other quotations from the Revised Standard Version are copyright 1946, 1952, by Division of Christian Education of the National Council of the Churches of Christ in the United States of America.

CHAPTER III • *Tabernacles and Me*

Mark 9:2-8. (King James Version.)

Matthew 16:16. (K.J.V.)

Mark 14:71. (K.J.V.)

Chorus of "He Loves Me, Too" by S. W. Straub. In *Worship and Conduct Songs,* edited by Elizabeth McE. Shields. Copyright, 1929, by Presbyterian Committee of Publication, Richmond, Virginia. (Punctuation changed slightly.)

Matthew 19:14. (R.S.V.)

Matthew 6:9. (R.S.V.)

Matthew 6:13. (R.S.V. footnote)

CHAPTER IV • *Me? Grow Up?*

John 21:15-17. (R.S.V.)

1 Corinthians 13:11. (K.J.V.)

1 Corinthians 3:2. (R.S.V.)

Matthew 4:19. (K.J.V. and R.S.V.)
See John 21:17. (R.S.V.)

CHAPTER V • *Me and My House*

Joshua 24:15. (R.S.V.)

CHAPTER VI • *My Church—His Body*

John 15:16. (K.J.V.)
Matthew 18:20. (K.J.V.)
Matthew 7:7. (K.J.V.)
John 15:16. (K.J.V.)
John 15:5. (K.J.V.)

CHAPTER VII • *My Community—Where I Take Him*

Matthew 23:37. (K.J.V.)
1 Corinthians 8:9, 13. (K.J.V.)
Luke 10:29. (R.S.V.)
E. Stanley Jones, *Mastery*, 22 words from p. 74. Copyright 1955 by Pierce & Washabaugh. Used by permission of Abingdon Press.

CHAPTER VIII • *God's Interruptions*

Acts 3:1-9. (R.S.V.)

CHAPTER IX • *A Hatful of Joy*

John 15:11. (K.J.V.)
John 15:16. (K.J.V.)
Matthew 28:20. (K.J.V.)
Philippians 4:13. (K.J.V. and R.S.V.)

CHAPTER X • *Adventure Begun*

Matthew 6:9-13. (K.J.V.)
Psalm 23. (K.J.V.)